Nouns and Pronouns

Kara Murray

PowerKiDS press.

New York

Published in 2014 by The Rosen Publishing Group, Inc.
29 East 21st Street, New York, NY 10010

First Edition

Editor: Amelie von Zumbusch
Book Design: Colleen Bialecki

Photo Credits: Cover, p. 9 Digital Vision/Getty Images; p. 5 Sergey Nivens/Shutterstock.com; p. 6 Stockbyte/Thinkstock; p. 7 Andrey Bayda/Shutterstock.com; p. 11 Brand X Pictures/Thinkstock; p. 12 Tatyana Vychegzhanina/Shutterstock.com; p. 13 William Hart/Stone/Getty Images; p. 15 Jeff Greenough/ Blend Images/Getty Images; p. 16 iStockphoto/Thinkstock; p. 17 Scholastic Studio 10/Photolibrary/Getty Images; p. 18 Medioimages/Photodisc/Thinkstock; p. 19 Benjamin Rondel/The Image Bank/Getty Images; p. 20 Jon Feingersh/Blend Images/Getty Images.

Library of Congress Cataloging-in-Publication Data
Murray, Kara.
  Nouns and pronouns / By Kara Murray. — First Edition.
    pages cm. — (Core Language Skills)
  Includes index.
  ISBN 978-1-4777-0800-2 (library binding) — ISBN 978-1-4777-0972-6 (pbk.) —
ISBN 978-1-4777-0973-3 (6-pack)
  1. English language—Noun—Juvenile literature. 2. English language—Pronoun—Juvenile literature.
3. English language—Parts of speech—Juvenile literature. I. Title.
  PE1201.M87 2014
  428.2—dc23
                                          201204677

Manufactured in the United States of America

CPSIA Compliance Information: Batch #S13PK5: For Further Information contact Rosen Publishing, New York, New York at 1-800-237-9932

Contents

Nouns and Pronouns

Take a look around you. What do you see? Anything that you can see, smell, touch, or hear is a noun. A noun is a person, place, or thing. Pronouns are words that can be used in place of nouns. They help keep us from repeating words and names. They are like shortcuts in language!

Pronouns help make our language more efficient. For example, you could write, "Sheila likes Mark." If you have already been writing about Sheila and Mark, though, you could also write, "She likes him." However, it needs to be clear what nouns pronouns **refer** to.

This is Jack. He has a dog. "Jack" and "dog" are nouns. "He" is a pronoun.

(See answers on p. 22)

FIGURE IT OUT

Can you identify the nouns and pronouns in the following sentences?

The team has one girl. She plays third base.

Kinds of Nouns

Common nouns are words used for people, places, things, or ideas. "Boy," "school," "kindness," and "squirrel" are common nouns. Proper nouns are the names of specific people or things. "Diego" and "Lassie" are proper nouns. The names of places are also proper nouns. This includes the names of countries, states, towns, and cities.

The words for states of being, such as "happiness," are nouns. Happiness is the state of being happy.

Times Square is in New York City. Since they are specific places, both "Times Square" and "New York City" are proper nouns.

Sometimes a proper noun and a common noun describe the same thing. "Store" is a common noun, but "Macy's" is a proper noun. How can you tell common and proper nouns apart? Proper nouns are always **capitalized**. Common nouns are capitalized only when they begin sentences.

FIGURE IT OUT

Can you identify the common and proper nouns in the following sentences?

Laura and Liz moved here from another state. The girls are from California.

See answers on p. 22)

One or More

Nouns can be **singular** or **plural**. The singular is used for just one. The plural is for more than one. Singular nouns called collective nouns refer to groups as a whole. Some examples are "army" and "herd."

You form the plural of most nouns by adding "s" or "es." The plural of "cat" is "cats." The plural of "box" is "boxes." These are **regular** plurals.

Chart of Singular and Plural Nouns

Singular	Plural
Baby	Babies
Cup	Cups
Potato	Potatoes
Toy	Toys
Watch	Watches
Wolf	Wolves

This girl is trying on dresses. To make words that end in "s" plural, you add the letters "es." You also add "es" to make words that end in "ch," "sh," and "x" plural.

Some nouns form plurals in different ways, though. These are **irregular** plurals. For example, "man" becomes "men," "child" becomes "children," and "mouse" becomes "mice." Some nouns are the same in singular and plural. These include "fish" and "deer."

FIGURE IT OUT

What are the plural forms of the following words?

Bus
Boat
Hat

See answers on p. 22)

You need to know if your nouns are singular or plural so that you know what **verb** form to use. A plural noun needs a plural verb. For example, read this sentence:

The river flows to the sea.

Here it is in plural form:

The rivers flow to the sea.

When using plural pronouns, you also need to use the plural verb form. Look at the following sentences:

The ants are busy. They are digging.

Both "ants" and "they" take plural verbs. A pronoun's number must also match the noun it refers to. "They" is plural because it refers to "ants."

"Team" is a collective noun, so it takes a singular verb form. It is correct to say "Our team always plays well."

FIGURE IT OUT

Change the following two sentences to make them plural.

A bear eats salmon.

A beaver makes a dam.

(See answers on p. 22)

Forming the Possessive

Sometimes, you might want to describe something that a person or thing possesses, or has. To show that a noun possesses something, use its possessive form.

You form the possessive of a singular noun by adding an **apostrophe** followed by an "s." One thing that a person possesses is hair. Let's say your friend Angela has red hair. Using the possessive, you could write, "Angela's hair is red."

Emma's bike is brand new. "Emma's" is the possessive form of the name "Emma." What is the possessive form of your name?

The possessive of plural nouns that end in "s" is formed simply by adding an apostrophe. Let's say you see some parrots with beautiful colors. To describe them using the possessive, write, "The parrots' colors are beautiful."

It is correct to write "The twins' room has a bunk bed." The word "twins" needs only an apostrophe on the end to make it possessive.

FIGURE IT OUT

How would you rewrite the following sentences using the possessive?

My brother has a red hat.

Our neighbors have a new car.

See answers on p. 22)

All Kinds of Pronouns

There are many kinds of pronouns. Some refer to unnamed people and things. These include "everybody," "anybody, "somebody," "all," "each," "some," "none," and "one."

Other pronouns refer to named people and their possessions. To refer to yourself, use "I" or "me." Use "my" or "mine" to refer to things that you have. To refer to another person or thing, use "he," "she," or "it." To refer to things that a person or thing owns, use "his," "her," "hers," or "its." To refer to other people or things, use "they" or "them." Use "their" or "theirs" to refer to multiple people's possessions.

It is Briana's turn in the game she is playing with her brother. If their dad asked whose turn it is, her answer would be "It's my turn!"

FIGURE IT OUT

Can you rewrite the following sentences using "he," then using "she," and finally using "they"?

I got a bike for my birthday. My new bike is red.

(See answers on p. 22)

One and the Same

There are certain pronouns that refer back to themselves. In the singular form, they include "myself," "yourself,' "himself," "herself," and "itself." In the plural, they are "ourselves," "yourselves," and "themselves."

This kind of pronoun is the **object** of a sentence. Objects are nouns or pronouns that receive a sentence's action. **Subjects** are nouns or pronouns that carry out that action. You use pronouns ending in "self" or "selves" when a sentence's object and subject refer to the same person or thing.

This cat is hiding itself behind some grass.

This boy is making himself breakfast. The pronoun "himself" can be used to draw attention to the fact a boy or man did something on his own.

Think about the sentence "I looked at myself in the mirror." In it, "I" and "myself" refer to the same person.

FIGURE IT OUT

Read the sentence "You looked at yourself in the mirror." Can you rewrite it with "the girl" as its subject?

See answers on p. 22)

Noun Clues

You may have noticed that some nouns seem to be two words in one. These are **compound** nouns. Even if a compound word is unfamiliar, you can often figure out what it means by breaking it up into its parts. For example, a "sunrise" is when the Sun rises in the sky at the beginning of a day.

"Birdhouse" is a compound noun. As you could likely guess, it is a house for a bird to live in.

Look at the sentence "My family played pétanque last Sunday." Even if you do not know what pétanque is, the word "played" gives you a clue that it is likely a game.

Other times, it may be harder to figure out a word's meaning just by breaking it into parts. This is when you can use **context**. Context is the words around a word that make that word's meaning clearer.

FIGURE IT OUT

Can you figure out what the italicized words in the sentence below mean?

The *bluebird* flew into the *greenhouse* to eat the berries on the plants growing there.

See answers on p. 22)

New Nouns

One of the great things about reading is that it introduces you to new words. Even adults come across new nouns while they are reading.

There are many tools that you can use to help you find a new noun's meaning. Try to have a **dictionary** near you while reading. A dictionary will list most English words, with pronunciation guides and definitions. If you don't have a print dictionary, you can use an online one. **Thesauruses** are useful as well. They show you words that have similar meanings to the one you are looking up. Learning new nouns is fun!

Libraries are a good place to find dictionaries. They often have really big dictionaries that have tens of thousands of words in them.

Use a dictionary to figure out what the following nouns mean:

Ibex
Quince

(See answers on p. 22)

Figure It Out: The Answers

Page 5: The nouns are "team," "girl," and "base." The pronoun is "she."

Page 7: The common nouns are "state" and "girls." The proper nouns are "Laura," Liz," and "California."

Page 9: The plurals are "buses," "boats," and "hats."

Page 11: The plural of the first sentence is "Bears eat salmon." The second sentence should be "Beavers make dams."

Page 13: The first sentence should read, "My brother's hat is red." The second sentence should read, "Our neighbors' car is new."

Page 15: The sentences using "he" should read, "He got a bike for his birthday. His new bike is red." The ones with "she" should read, "She got a bike for her birthday. Her new bike is red." Using "they," the sentences should read, "They got new bikes for their birthdays. Their new bikes are red."

Page 17: The sentence should read, "The girl looked at herself in the mirror."

Page 19: A bluebird is a kind of bird that is blue. You can guess this by breaking "bluebird" into "blue" and "bird." A greenhouse is a building where plants are grown. This word's meaning is a little trickier to figure out. The two parts of "greenhouse" are "green" and "house." Using context, though, it doesn't seem likely that the word means simply a house that is green. Context is also what tells us that there are plants growing in the greenhouse.

Page 21: An ibex is a kind of wild goat. A quince is an applelike fruit or the tree on which that fruit grows.

apostrophe (uh-POS-truh-fee) A punctuation mark that looks like this: '.

capitalized (KA-pih-tuh-lyzd) Starting with a capital, or uppercase, letter.

compound (KOM-pownd) Having two or more things put together.

context (KON-tekst) Words around a word that make that word's meaning clearer.

dictionary (DIK-shuh-ner-ee) A book that lists words alphabetically and explains their meanings.

irregular (ih-REH-gyuh-lur) Not made or done in the usual way.

object (OB-jekt) A noun or pronoun that receives the action of a sentence.

plural (PLUR-el) Having to do with more than one.

refer (rih-FUR) To speak of or have to do with.

regular (REH-gyuh-lur) Made or done in the usual way.

singular (SIN-gyuh-lur) Having to do with just one.

subjects (SUB-jiktz) Nouns or pronouns that carry out the action in a sentence.

thesauruses (thih-SOR-us-ez) Books that list words that are alike and words that are different from each other.

verb (VERB) A word that describes an action.

Index

Websites

Due to the changing nature of Internet links, PowerKids Press has developed an online list of websites related to the subject of this book. This site is updated regularly. Please use this link to access the list:
www.powerkidslinks.com/cls/noun/